EMOTIONINK

*Kickstart
Your Sobriety by
Journalizing Your
First 30-Days*

FRANK GARCIA

THE AUTHOR OF REFURBISHED SOUL

ISBN: 978-0-9600633-1-4

"

It's a wondrous thing, that a decision to act releases energy in the personality. For days on end a person may drift along without much energy. Having no particular sense of direction and having no will to change. Then, something happens to alter the pattern. It may be something very simple and inconsequential. But it stabs awake, it alarms, it disturbs. In a flash, one gets a vivid picture of oneself, and it passes. The result is decision. Sharp, definitive decision. In the wake of the decision, yes, even as a part of the decision itself, energy is released. The act of decision sweeps all before it, and the life of the individual may be changed forever.

—HOWARD THURMAN

"

If you don't listen, YOU WILL!

— M e

I REPEAT THIS QUOTE *ALL the time.*

Over the years, people have asked me, "what does that mean?" The answer is always the same, though not quite as simple.

With almost every thought, we have a sense of direction. It is an internal instinct that is supposed to guide our choices. The road ahead always branches in multiple directions; one is a more challenging path and the other *appears* easier and seems to promise the same result/reward as the first. *That is just an illusion.*

Our sense of direction usually tells us that, just as in the Robert Frost poem, we should choose "the road less traveled," even though it is the more challenging path. We hear voices that guide us in that direction, too, both in our minds and from those around us. However, too many times we choose to take the easy route. Because it is *easier*, right?

We usually find out that the "voices" were right. We should have listened to them.

In the end, I learned through hard experience that by *not* listening to the voices—the *voices of reason*—I ended up paying a greater price mentally, physically, and psychologically. Of course, like many I complained, "why did this happen *to* me?" But that complaint just is not valid. Nothing happened *to* me. It all happened *because* of me.

If you dig deep enough, and really pay attention, you will always know which direction is the best, wisest path. I highly advise you to listen to your voices.

Because if you don't, YOU WILL. Learning this lesson, the hard way can be a painful price to pay.

Your Sobriety Journal

Introduction

HELLO! THANK YOU SO MUCH for picking up the *Emotionink* **journal to recovery**. I wrote this journal with the upmost respect for you, your time, and your path to recovery. I intentionally kept its information short and sweet without any fluff. Fluff is not what you need right now.

The whole idea of this journal was to provide you with a short, usable blueprint to help you reprogram your brain, rebuild your character, and come face to face with all the emotions running through you.

With the *Emotionink* Journal, you can begin your first step towards *your better self*.

By now, you have realized that before today, your past life just wasn't for you. You have recognized that reaching your **personal rock bottom** is not the path that you choose to continue. You have flipped off the mirror one too many times and realize that a change is needed, and no, not later, it is required right now. The title of the Journal is whatever you personally want it to be. I chose *Emotionink* because for a long time now, my journey, my poetry, short stories, and book were supported by my emotions. I invite you each day to not be afraid of your emotions, no matter if they are right, wrong, or make you feel vulnerable. Reintroduce yourself to them, and together you will break down mental boundaries.

1

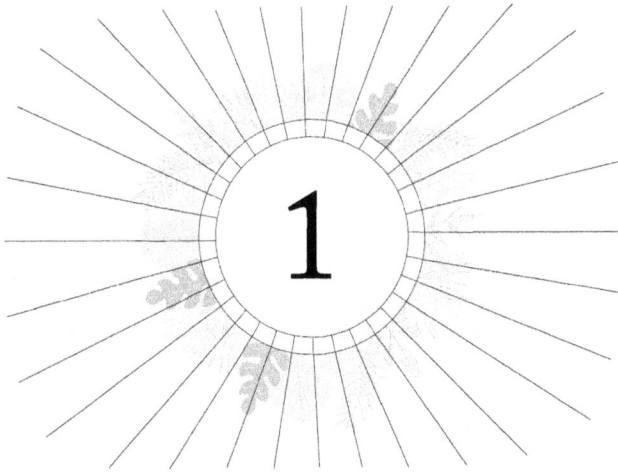

Are recovery programs right for YOU?

YES!

Now, that does not mean that every recovery plan works for every person. You may need to go through more than one recovery plan to find one what works for you. Full disclosure: after I went to rehab, I was drinking again within 60 days. Was that the rehabilitation center's fault? No. It was **my** fault, *one hundred percent*, because I did not adhere to the program's lessons and allow them to take a deep enough root.

Second, I grew tired of group sessions because I witnessed people constantly coming in drunk or high every visit. Their romanticizing of their past drove me up the wall. What I perceived as their failures laid the groundwork for my own.

It took me three different Intensive Outpatient Programs (IOP) to confirm that they, too, did not work for me.

Everyone is different. Maybe it is because I'm stubborn, but I needed to white-knuckle my way through. That made the process extremely tough, but it seems that is how *I* learn. I had no personal support to lean on; no one I knew had been through what I was going through. That meant going solo was what I needed to do.

Please take note: I *do not* recommend tackling your sobriety alone. Reach out to as many people as you can. The right support can help you set the foundation you need to build a strong and healthy recovery plan that works for you.

2

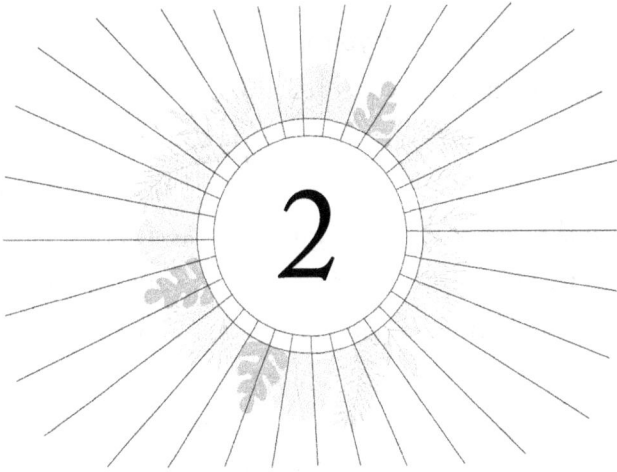

How to make the best use of this 30-day Journal.

FROM THE FIRST DAY YOU COMMIT to getting clean and sober you must come to terms with a brutal fact: *your body still wants to be in charge.* DO NOT let it. From today forward, you need to start making micro adjustments to your mentality. Ultimately, that is what will reintroduce you to the happy and healthy side of you. It is still in there, waiting… not always patiently.

Each lined page in your journal lists the numbered day you are on and asks you the all-important question: *"How am I feeling and do these feelings deserve my attention?*

I recommend that you immediately write down the answer—describe how you are feeling. It doesn't have to be neat or even in any specific sequence. The idea here is just to *write your feelings down*. When you have done that, go back and **authorize yourself** to give *only* the feelings that you see as healthy permission to remain in your mindset. Take the time and **circle** the good feelings you wish to maintain and draw a straight line through the feelings that must go!

Yes, surprising as that may seem, you need to *give yourself permission* to only allow the good feelings to take root during your days of transformation. For example, if I wrote that I was angry, sad, depressed, and hopeful, afterwards I would only *allow* the "hopeful" feeling to take root and journey with me through my day. By doing this every day, you begin to see yourself regaining control of the positive person you once lost. The more of these days you have, the better. You will soon become accustomed to only allowing these positive feelings in. That will allow you to own every moment within your day.

3

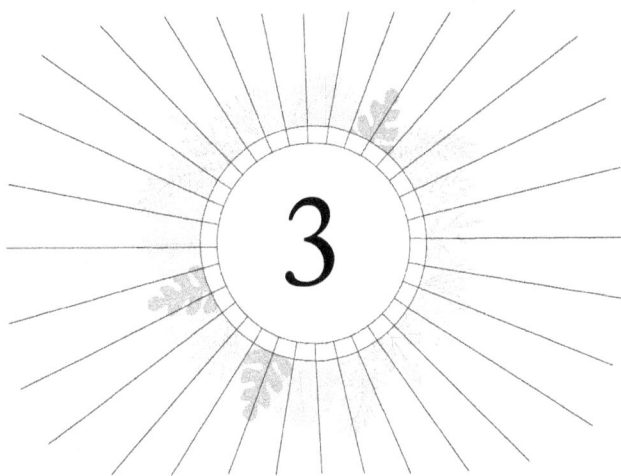

Understanding your past and present behaviors.

INTIMATELY UNDERSTANDING YOUR PAST CAN help guide your future. You may say, "Well, Frank, I have a pretty messed up past. How can that help me?" The answer is simple: **people who do not understand or respect their past are destined to repeat the poor behaviors they are trying to change.** One of the biggest character-building things we can do is recognize any and all ill-behaviors and commit to changing them going forward.

You see, the people around you have grown to only see you as you were: a drunk, a druggy, a deadbeat and or any other unflattering descriptions that we *earned* for doing what we did. Once you show them a different person, your true person inside, their perceptions of you will change. But to make that happen, you first need to *change your own perception* of who you are. From today forward you need to recognize that the majority of what you did was NOT a "mistake," it was a BAD DECISION.

I can tell you from personal experience that the day you make this statement part of who you are, *you will begin to feel a sense of freedom, self-forgiveness, and growth.*

Our past, like the review mirror in a car, is only meant to be checked occasionally. Like driving a car, we cannot go forward if we are always looking in the rearview. This means that as you trek forward towards your "new you," a refurbished character of good, do not dwell on what you went through in past; simply recognize it and respect it but *don't* pretend that it wasn't you.

As you grow, this mindset will empower you to become mentally strong, nonmalleable, and unbreakable. Always remember, where the mind goes, the body will follow.

4

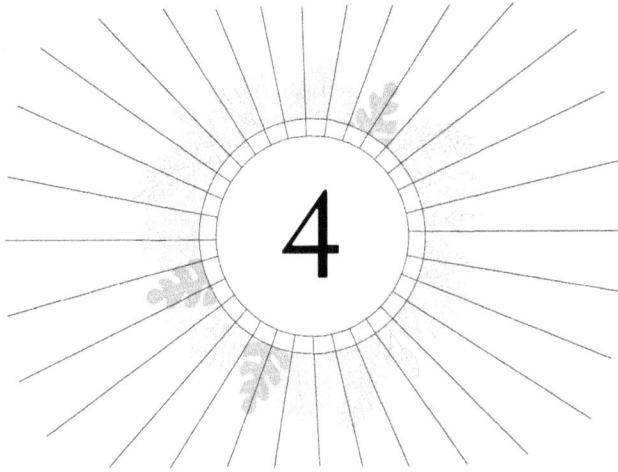

Making the personal commitment to change.

"It is not the strongest of the species that survives, nor the most intelligent that survives. It is the one that is most adaptable to change."

—CHARLES DARWIN

DURING YOUR TREK FORWARD, YOU will begin to see that CHANGE is needed and that it is mandatory to retrain the way you do things. Change, from today onward, will become your new "normal." When you see these changes become new habits... well, then you are witnessing internal and external progress. This progress will not be easy, but always remember that all rewarding changes in one's life take hard work.

5

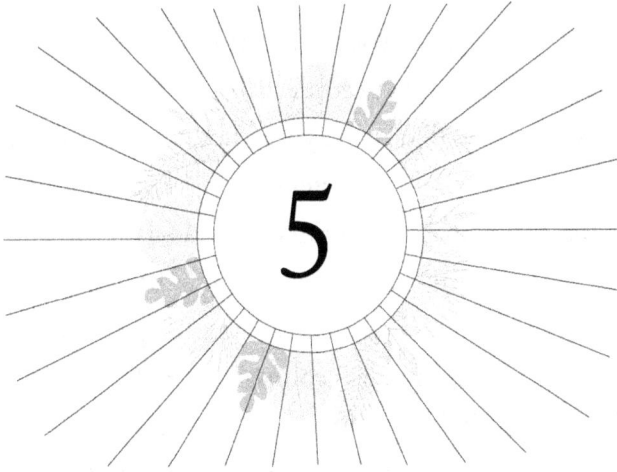

Become the expert on you.

THE FIRST THING TO DO here is recognize that *now you are on a beneficial path to become free of your old addictive self.* When you do that, you can welcome in personal and mental freedom. Most would agree that many people are completely unaware whether they are on a harmful or beneficial path. They likely think, "If I am not harming myself or others, well, I must be doing something right."

That is how we got the term "Ignorance is Bliss." That doesn't make it right, obviously. You cannot change something you do not know exists. You need to become an expert on what or where you are heading and *go all in on you.*

I would ask you to recognize *why* becoming a self-expert is critical. When you grow into the big shoes of becoming your own self-expert, you will start devoting your time to learning about yourself on many intimate levels. All your actions begin to align with your thoughts, and you begin to witness that self-improvement is becoming a way of life.

One can ask, "Well, Frank how do I become a self-expert?" To do that, you must become best friends with your self-awareness. Personally, when I began my clean & sober path, I held myself accountable for all my actions on almost an hourly level.

Now, some could say, "Wow Frank, that sounds excessive?" Yes. Yes, it is. But for me, wanting the freedom from drugs and alcohol so badly, I saw nothing as "excessive"—only progressive. *Self-awareness also begins right here with this journal* because here you will begin to acknowledge both emotions and feelings to help chart out your next thought and or move.

6

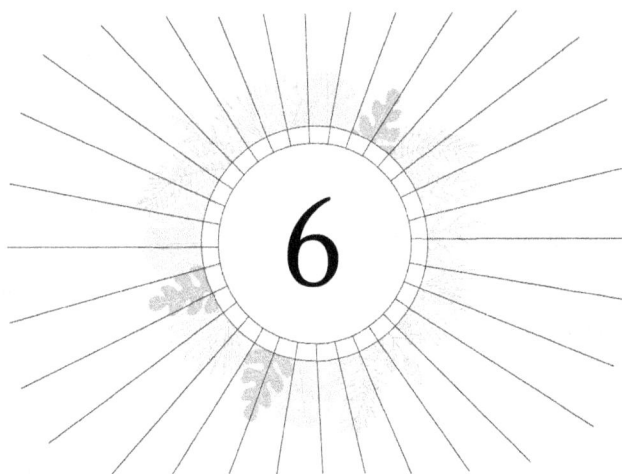

Recognizing your triggers and reprogramming the brain.

> *Habit: an acquired behavior pattern regularly followed until it has become almost involuntary. A dominant or regular disposition or tendency; prevailing character or quality.*
>
> —DICTIONARY.COM

ALWAYS LISTEN TO YOUR MIND, BODY, AND soul. One of the best ways to recognize your triggers is by paying close attention to your inner emotions and how a situation makes you feel and think. Yes, this is all part of the self-awareness we touched upon earlier. When you become hyper-aware of these moments, you begin retraining your brain's limbic response to things.

Next, teach yourself to either mentally or physically *take a step back*. Access what is happening, authorize its validity within your life, and process it accordingly. As you begin to notice these signs more quickly, **journalize** them, review these instances often, and become more comfortable with your plan of attack.

Somewhere in your new journal you **should** identify your **top three emotional triggers** which cause you imbalance or hardship and keep them closer to you than away. In due time, you will realize they no longer have any power over you.

When it comes to "retraining" your brain, you must first understand that when the limbic system is impaired (like from drinking too much and doing drugs), it will not function properly. When this happens, the rest of our body's systems feel the wrath. As I learned firsthand, as your body begins to react you will notice dysfunctions within your immune system, overall mood, digestion (or lack thereof), poor memory, and a sense of being dazed.

I strongly advise that as you begin to retrain your brain, start the process slowly by altering current habits that you grew up with. For example, when I began to retrain my brain, I started by:

- ► Eating with the opposite hand.
- ► Brushing my teeth with the opposite hand.
- ► Tying my shoes left over right because I grew up right over left.
- ► No longer drinking coffee (for one year).
- ► No longer eating meat (forever).
- ► Changing the TV channel with opposite hand (I don't even watch TV anymore).

I think you get the point. I chose common things that my brain and body were used to doing without even thinking. I altered their pattern of travel within my brain. You might ask, "What does that do, Frank?" Well, by reprogramming how I **did** things, I was able to set the new standard for how I **do** things. Second, all these small changes enabled me to detour my thoughts and focus from drugs and alcohol over to my new daily "norms." Yes, that is right; it was such a challenge altering these old habits, that it literally took my mind elsewhere each day.

7

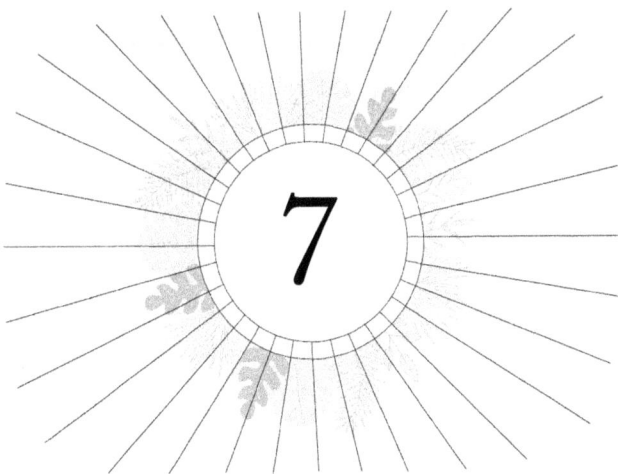

"You must unlearn what you have learned."

It is the classic quote from Yoda. During the movie "The Empire Strikes Back" he is training an exasperated Luke Skywalker who says something is too difficult for him to do. What the little Jedi Master explains in this scene is that the moment that you think or say the opposite of what you want to accomplish you actually begin to place limits on what you can physically accomplish. You basically pre-program yourself to fail.

We have all been taught to behave or act a certain way during our upbringing. It was through our alcoholism and addiction that we accepted these old behaviors as "normal."

But now we can begin to retrain that brain muscle and become free to alter how we think.

8

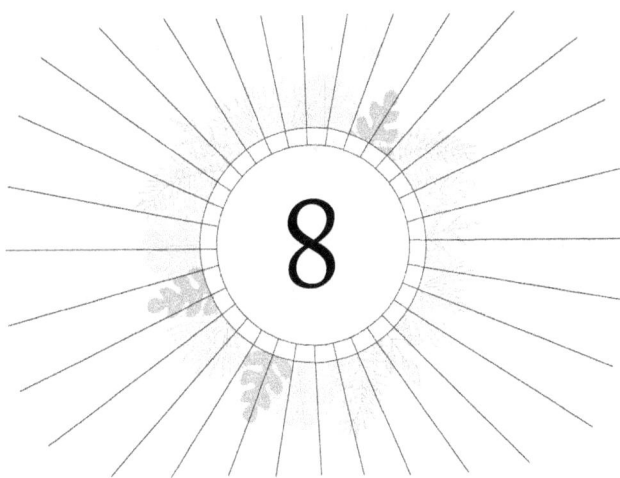

Your 30 day Journal

BEFORE YOU TURN TO THE next page of your journal, please accept the fact that you may not feel like writing each and every day for the next 30 days. But I am asking you to *trust in yourself and the process* and invite the face-to-face showdown with your emotions. After you have written down your emotions, go back and **circle what good you would like to retain**, and **cross out any negative emotions that you wish to go away**. That is correct: take your writing instrument and *draw a straight line across those ill emotions*. Be gone with them.

At the end of each day, you will begin to realize that any "bad" in that day really was not that bad. Even more empowering, all the good in that day was *your* creation because you produced a different mindset. Your manifestation first begins as a thought in your head and is then followed by your actions.

Stephen Covey once said, "Begin with the end in mind." This statement really aided me in my transformation; in fact, it still sticks with me today within my every thought. For example, in my book *Refurbished Soul* I talk about my WHY, what I VALUE and staying in ALIGNMENT. Together with Mr. Covey's statement, this practice will enable you to envision where you want to end up and recognize what proper decisions will help get you there.

Stay focused, write down everything you feel in your journal, and really envision the person you want to see in the mirror at the end of each day. You are 30 days away.

DAY 1

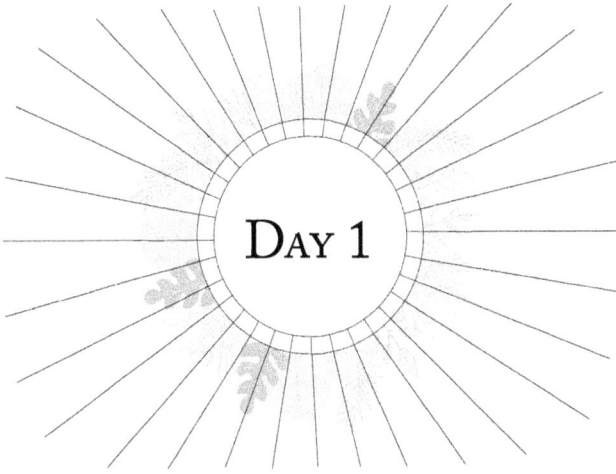

How am I feeling and do these
feelings deserve my attention?

_____

_____

_____

_____

_____

_____

_____

_____

_____

_____

_____

_____

_____

_____

_____

_____

_____

_____

Day 2

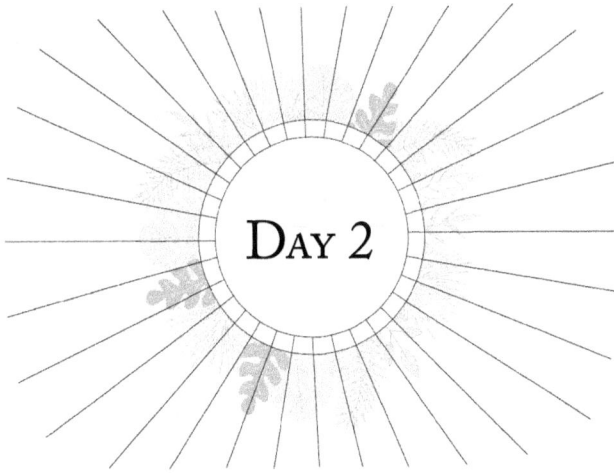

How am I feeling and do these feelings deserve my attention?

_____

_____

_____

_____

_____

_____

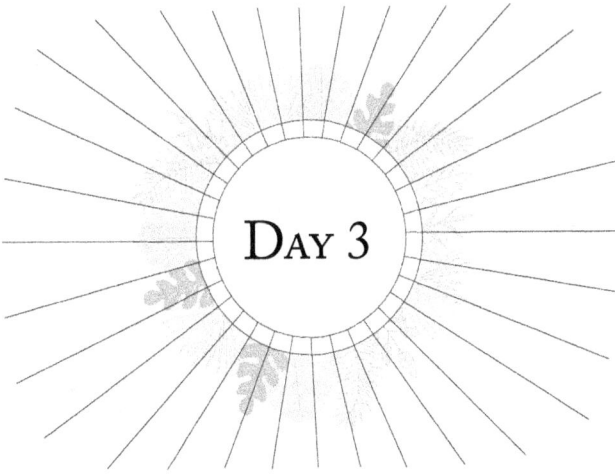

DAY 3

How am I feeling and do these feelings deserve my attention?

_____

_____

_____

_____

_____

_____

DAY 4

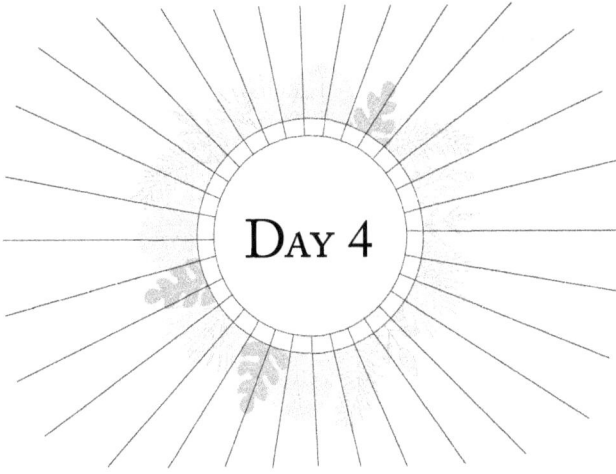

How am I feeling and do these feelings deserve my attention?

_____

_____

_____

_____

_____

_____

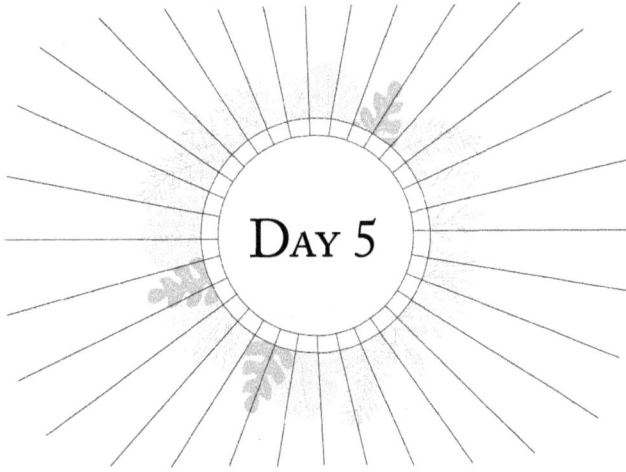

DAY 5

How am I feeling and do these feelings deserve my attention?

_____

_____

_____

_____

_____

_____

DAY 6

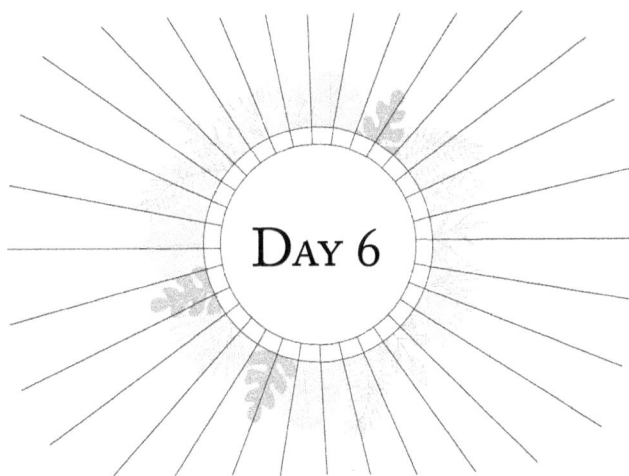

How am I feeling and do these feelings deserve my attention?

_____

_____

_____

_____

_____

_____

DAY 7

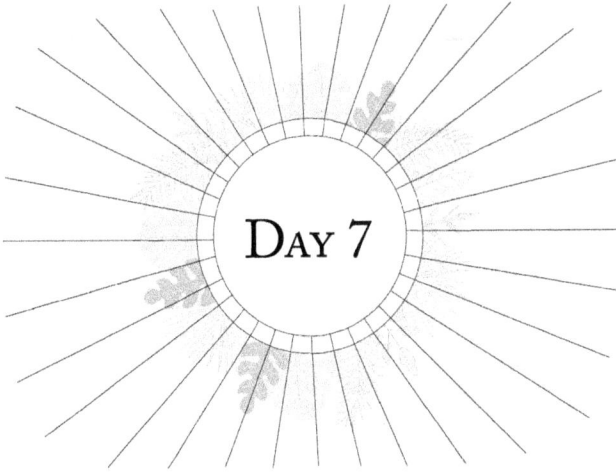

How am I feeling and do these feelings deserve my attention?

_____

_____

_____

_____

_____

_____

DAY 8

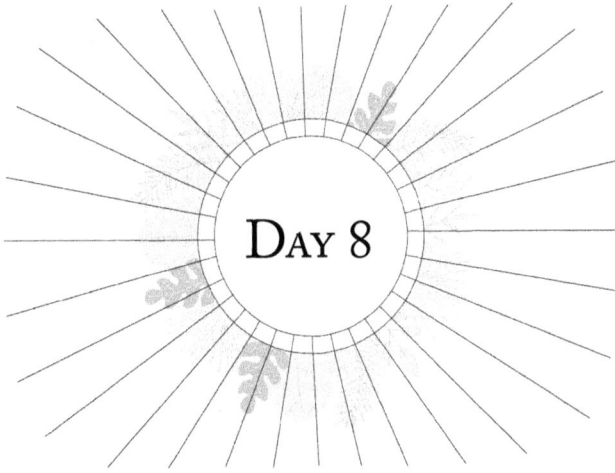

How am I feeling and do these feelings deserve my attention?

_____

_____

_____

_____

_____

_____

DAY 9

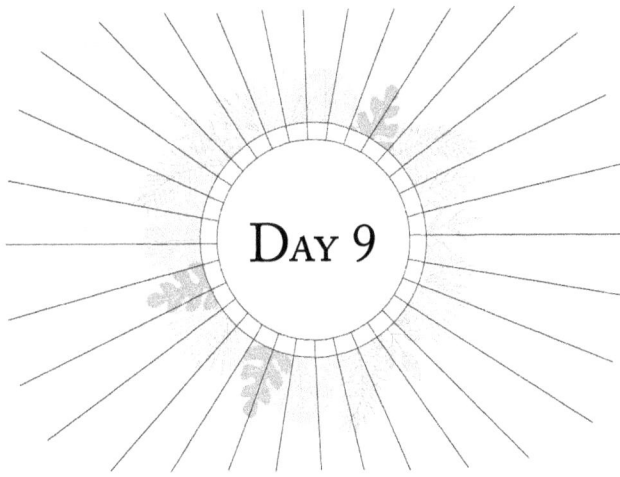

How am I feeling and do these feelings deserve my attention?

_____

_____

_____

_____

_____

_____

DAY 10

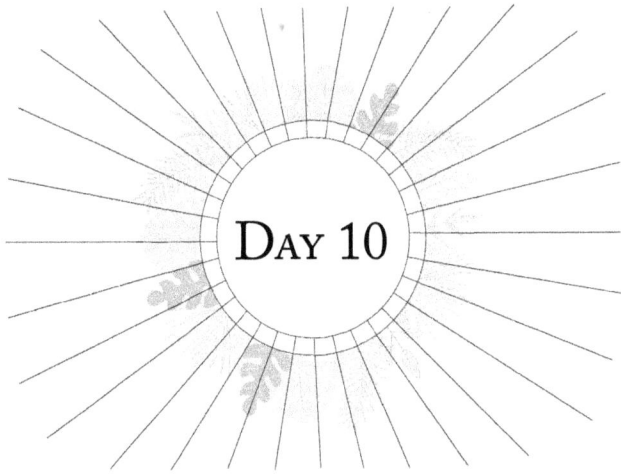

How am I feeling and do these feelings deserve my attention?

_____

_____

_____

_____

_____

_____

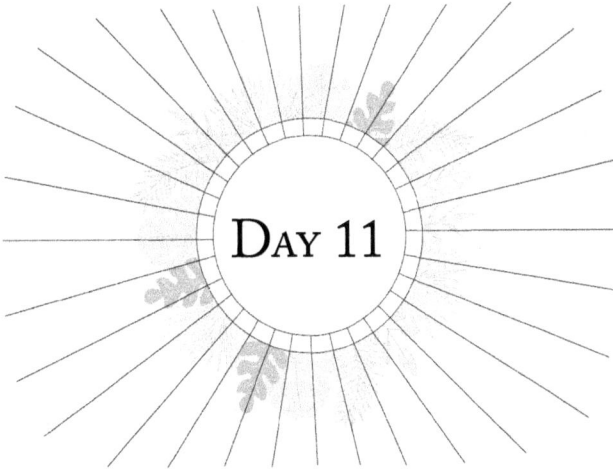

DAY 11

How am I feeling and do these feelings deserve my attention?

_____

_____

_____

_____

_____

_____

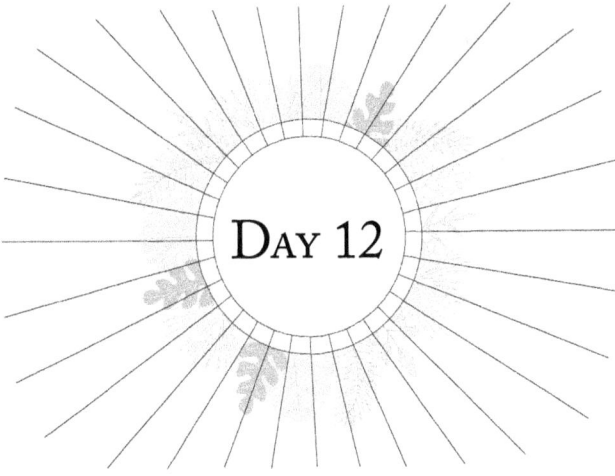

DAY 12

How am I feeling and do these feelings deserve my attention?

_____

_____

_____

_____

_____

_____

DAY 13

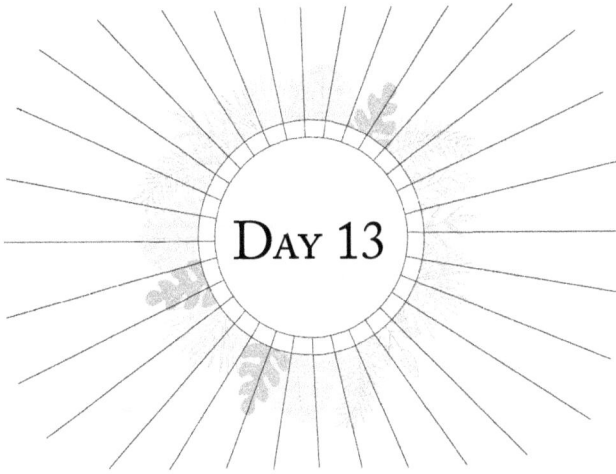

How am I feeling and do these feelings deserve my attention?

_____

_____

_____

_____

_____

_____

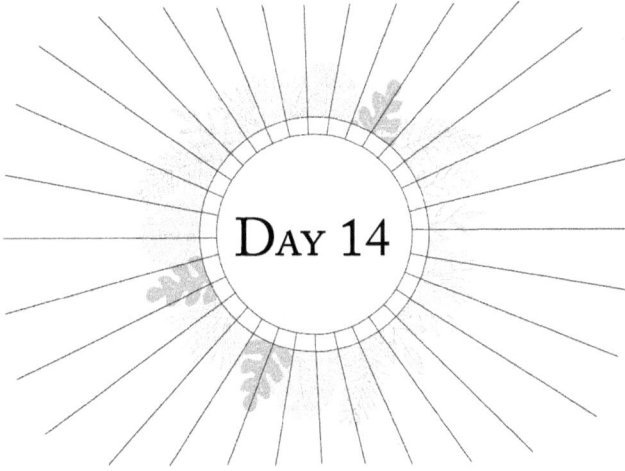

DAY 14

How am I feeling and do these feelings deserve my attention?

_____

_____

_____

_____

_____

_____

DAY 15

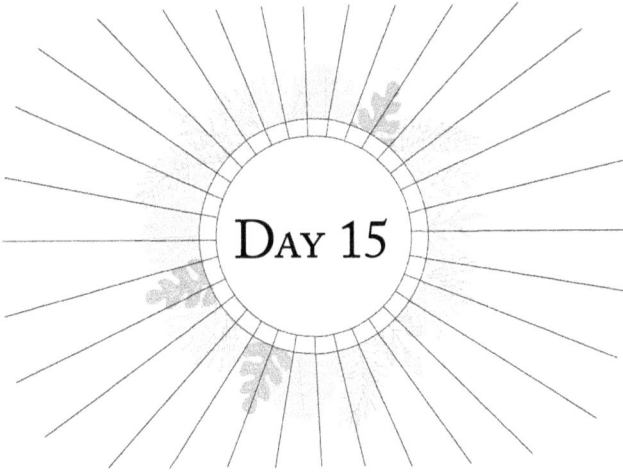

How am I feeling and do these feelings deserve my attention?

_____

_____

_____

_____

_____

_____

DAY 16

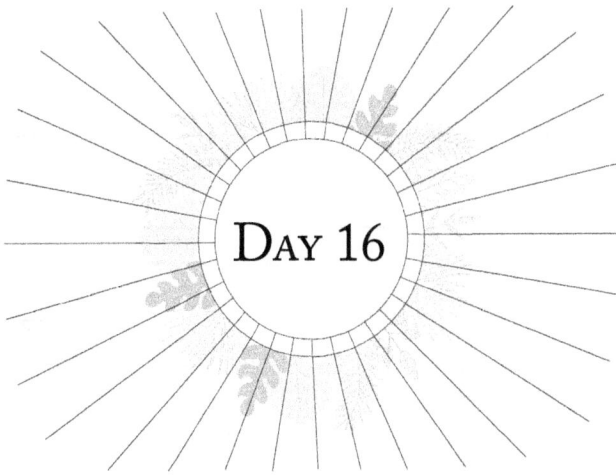

How am I feeling and do these feelings deserve my attention?

_____

_____

_____

_____

_____

_____

_____

_____

_____

_____

_____

_____

_____

_____

_____

_____

_____

_____

DAY 17

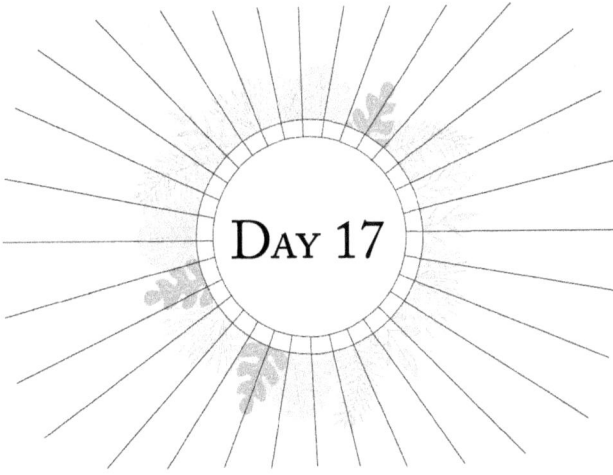

How am I feeling and do these feelings deserve my attention?

_____

_____

_____

_____

_____

_____

DAY 18

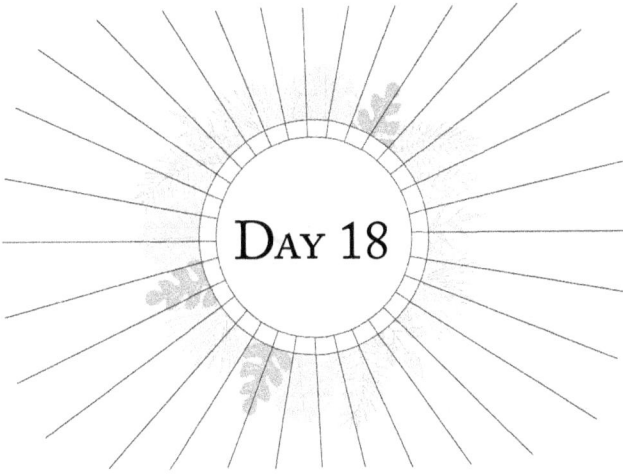

How am I feeling and do these feelings deserve my attention?

_____

_____

_____

_____

_____

_____

DAY 19

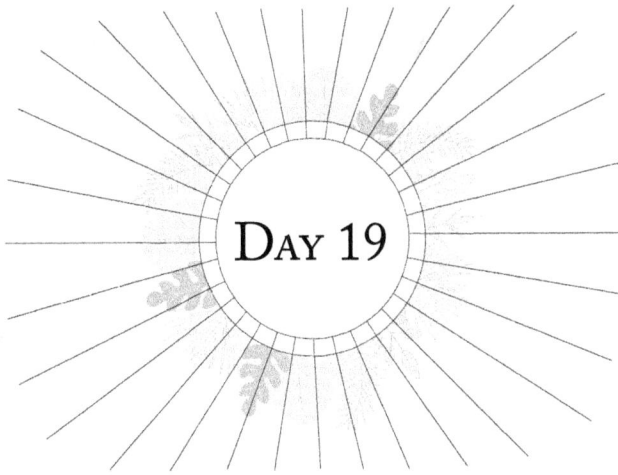

How am I feeling and do these feelings deserve my attention?

_____

_____

_____

_____

_____

_____

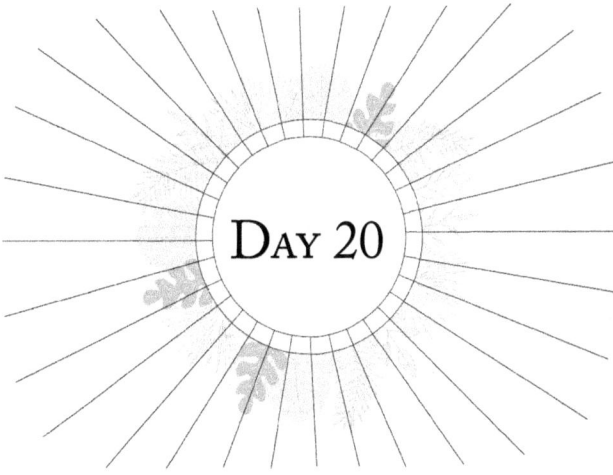

DAY 20

How am I feeling and do these feelings deserve my attention?

_____

_____

_____

_____

_____

_____

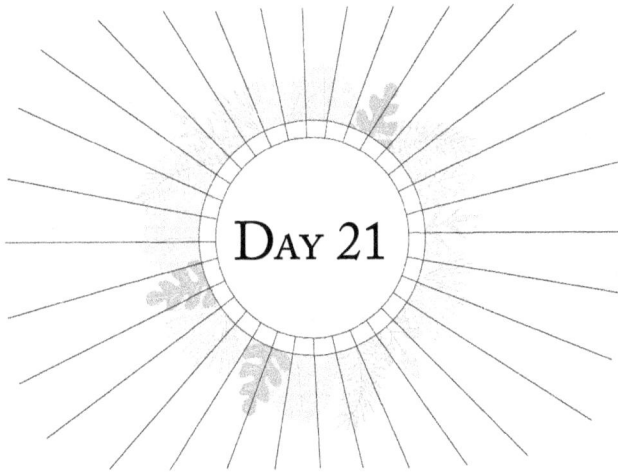

DAY 21

How am I feeling and do these feelings deserve my attention?

_____

_____

_____

_____

_____

_____

DAY 22

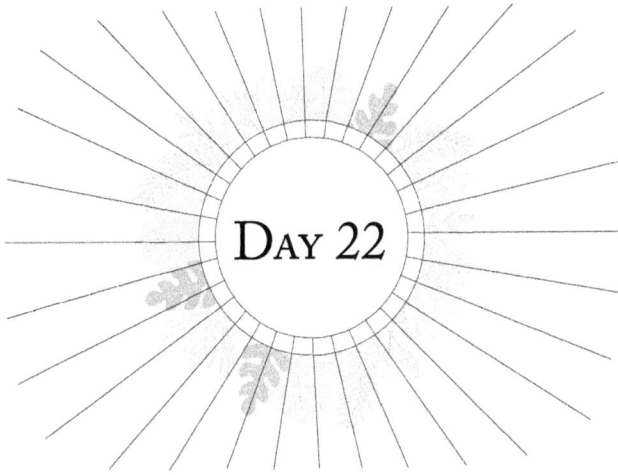

How am I feeling and do these feelings deserve my attention?

_____

_____

_____

_____

_____

_____

_____

_____

_____

_____

_____

_____

_____

_____

_____

_____

_____

_____

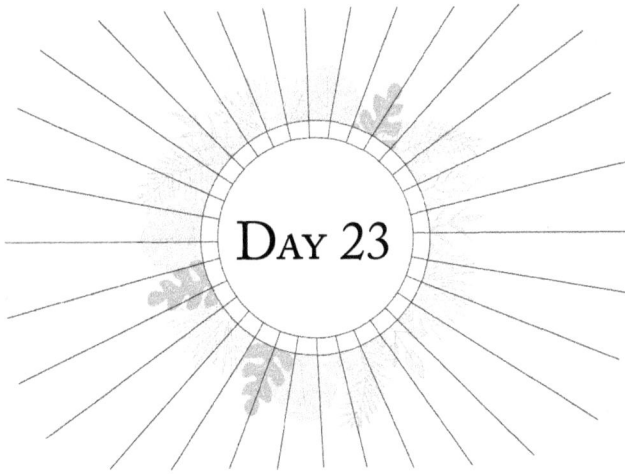

DAY 23

How am I feeling and do these feelings deserve my attention?

_____

_____

_____

_____

_____

_____

DAY 24

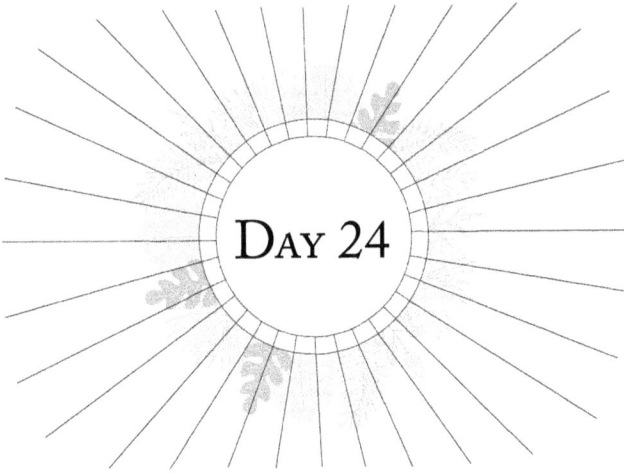

How am I feeling and do these feelings deserve my attention?

_____

_____

_____

_____

_____

_____

Day 25

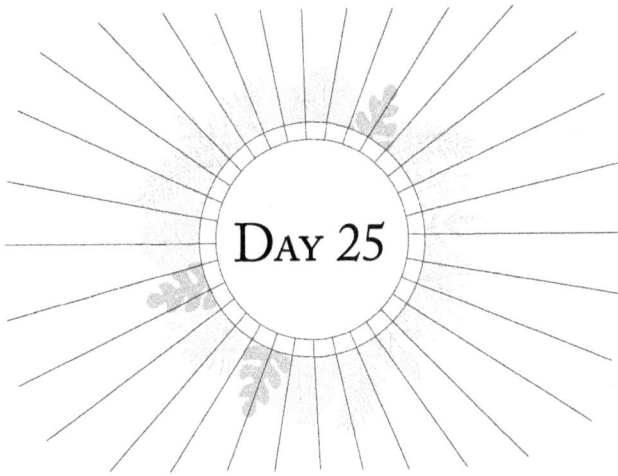

How am I feeling and do these feelings deserve my attention?

_____

_____

_____

_____

_____

_____

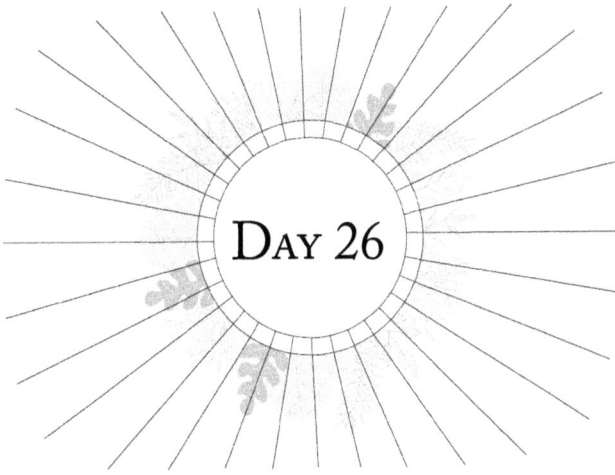

DAY 26

How am I feeling and do these feelings deserve my attention?

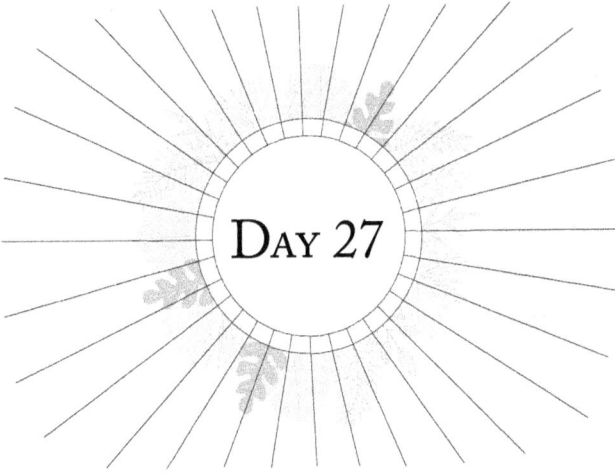

DAY 27

How am I feeling and do these feelings deserve my attention?

_____

_____

_____

_____

_____

_____

DAY 28

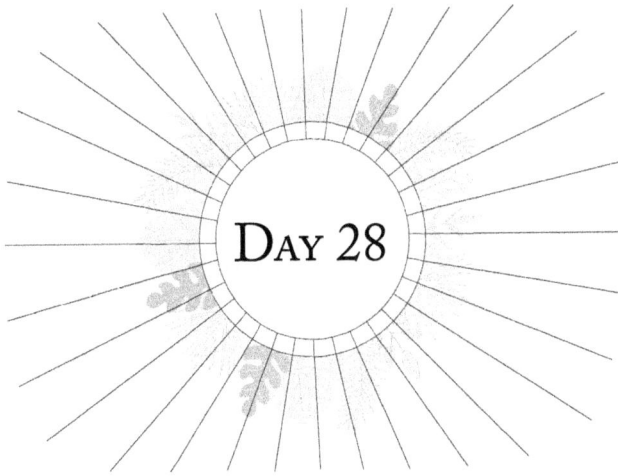

How am I feeling and do these feelings deserve my attention?

_____

_____

_____

_____

_____

_____

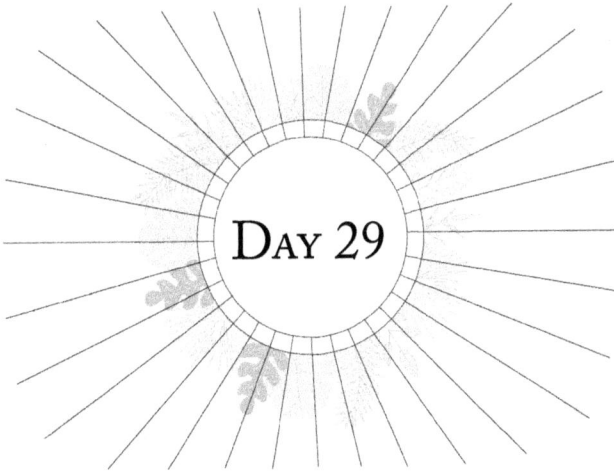

Day 29

How am I feeling and do these feelings deserve my attention?

_____

_____

_____

_____

_____

_____

DAY 30

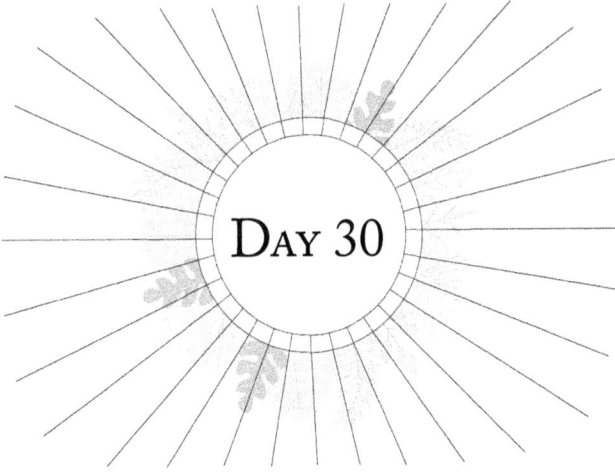

How am I feeling and do these feelings deserve my attention?

_____

_____

_____

_____

_____

_____

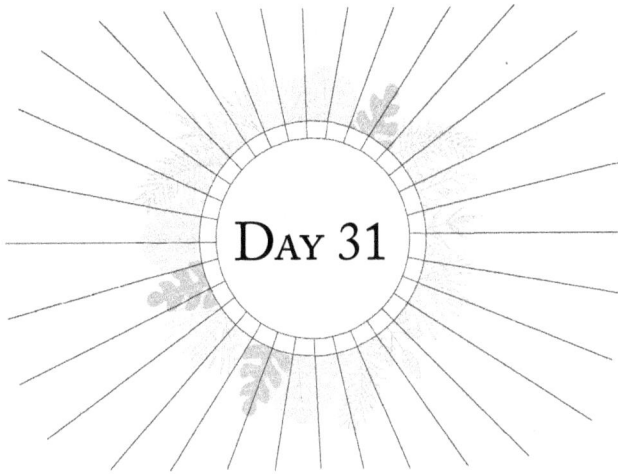

DAY 31

How am I feeling and do these feelings deserve my attention?

_____

_____

_____

_____

_____

_____

How are you feeling today?

BY NOW YOU HAVE WITNESSED a whirlwind of different emotions, feelings, mood swings, night sweats, anxieties, depressive states, guilt, hopelessness, *and* moments of joy. That's OK, *all of it*, and everything will continue to be okay as long you felt that each one of these emotions was valid and was confirmed by you in that moment.

Your body and emotional state had to go through these last 30 days to create the new foundation you need to stand tall and progress through your recovery. You did it!

Of course, you may be asking, "So, now what Frank?" My answer would be different for each one of you individually, but I will share a few ideas that can really help.

- ▶ Pick-up my book *Refurbished Soul* and read what has kept me unbreakable for 10 years now.

- ▶ Stay with a support group that adds to your life (but does not take away).

- ▶ If you started a step-program and it is working, DO NOT STOP applying it to your recovery.

- ► If you started an exercise program, DO NOT STOP exercising

- ► If you started reading motivational books, DO NOT STOP reading.

- ► If you have reconnected with loved ones, DO NOT STOP connecting.

- ► If you have started working harder, DO NOT STOP working harder.

- ► If you have told your significant other that you want another chance, DO NOT STOP *showing them* that you do. As Yoda would say, "Do. Or do not. There is no try."

I could go on and on, but as I said, I have extreme respect for your time (plus, you have already listened to me for the last 30 days)! Just remember, it does not end here. I strongly advise you to *keep reprogramming your brain*, stay focused on the results you envision and ***do not quit on yourself.***

I love each and every one of you.
All the best,
Frank

Now that you have completed your journal, please take a moment to leave me a review on Amazon and at www.refurbishedsoul.com/emotionink

Thank you.

www.ingramcontent.com/pod-product-compliance
Lightning Source LLC
Chambersburg PA
CBHW072045040426
42447CB00012BB/3026